NATURE TRAILS
— and —
GOSPEL TALES

Stories of Grace from the Wilds of Mississippi

ERNEST HERNDON

InterVarsity Press
Downers Grove, Illinois

InterVarsity Press
P.O. Box 1400, Downers Grove, IL 60515-1426
World Wide Web: www.ivpress.com
E-mail: mail@ivpress.com

InterVarsity Press® *is the book-publishing division of InterVarsity Christian Fellowship/USA*®*, a student movement active on campus at hundreds of universities, colleges and schools of nursing in the United States of America, and a member movement of the International Fellowship of Evangelical Students. For information about local and regional activities, write Public Relations Dept., InterVarsity Christian Fellowship/USA, 6400 Schroeder Rd., P.O. Box 7895, Madison, WI 53707-7895, or visit the IVCF website at <www.ivcf.org>.*

All Scripture quotations, unless otherwise indicated, are taken from the Holy Bible, New International Version®. NIV®. *Copyright* ©*1973, 1978, 1984 by International Bible Society. Used by permission of Zondervan Publishing House. All rights reserved.*

Design: Cindy Kiple
Cover Images: old boots: David Prince/Getty Images
             butterfly: Photodisc/Getty Images

Interior illustrations: Cindy Kiple

ISBN 0-8308-3236-X

Printed in Canada ∞

Library of Congress Cataloging-in-Publication Data

Herndon, Ernest.
  Nature trails and Gospel tales: stories of grace from the wilds of
Mississippi/J. Ernest Herndon.
     p. cm.
Includes bibliographical references.
  ISBN 0-8308-3236-X (cloth: alk. paper)
  1. Nature—Religious aspects—Christianity—Meditations. 2. Outdoor
life—Mississippi. I. Title.
  BT695.5.H47 2004
  277.62'082—dc22

                                                2003026437

P	15	14	13	12	11	10	9	8	7	6	5	4	3	2	1
Y	13	12	11	10	09	08	07	06	05	04					

I'd like to thank "Miss Mattie" Rials

for suggesting I write this book

and my wife, Angelyn, for insisting.

This book is dedicated

to my grandson

Andrew Wilson Coy

CONTENTS

PREFACE

The Greatest (Outdoor) Story Ever Told

At a small daily newspaper like the one where I work, it's not uncommon for writers to have many duties. For instance, I'm both outdoors editor and religion editor. That may seem a strange combination, especially when compared to larger newspapers where outdoors editors focus on hunting and fishing, religion editors write about churches and ministries, and ne'er the twain overlap. But I have found the two subjects to be perfectly compatible. Many Christians delight in the wonders of God's creation; many people who enjoy the outdoors appreciate the divine hand in nature.

The Bible itself is a great source of nature writing, from beginning to end. You might call it the greatest outdoor story ever told. The Good Book is full of hunters, fishermen, campers, hikers and boaters. It contains the most beautiful nature poetry ever written. And its adventure stories are unparalleled. Where else do you find a fish catching a man (Jonah) rather than vice versa?

Things get intriguing right off the bat when Genesis 2:10-14 maps out the Garden of Eden. "A river watering the garden flowed from Eden; from there it was separated into four headwaters," says Genesis 2:10, going on to list the Tigris and Euphrates, which are identifiable today, and the Pishon and Gihon, which are not.

The wording sets up a mystery: Are those four branches upstream or downstream of Eden? In other words, does the river flow out of Eden and then split, or do the four headwaters merge to form the river that flows through Eden? Commentators come up with a wide range of interpretations, some claiming Eden reached as far as India and Ethiopia, others saying it was concentrated in present-day Iraq. As one who has gotten turned around in Louisiana's Honey Island Swamp, where the Pearl River splits into approximately five branches, I take particular interest in the Eden river situation.

The Old Testament continues with stories of outdoorsmen and women like Nimrod, Noah, Abraham, Hagar, Esau, Moses, Deborah, Samson, Ruth, Naomi, David and Elijah, culminating with magnificent nature poetry in books like Psalms, Job and Isaiah. Consider passages like Psalm 19, which begins,

> The heavens declare the glory of God;
>> the skies proclaim the work of his hands.

Or Psalm 104:

> How many are your works, O LORD!
>> In wisdom you made them all;
>> the earth is full of your creatures. (v. 24)

Especially stirring is Job 38—41, when "the LORD answered Job out of the storm" and described the marvels of creation. Weary of the endless haggling of Job and his friends, God says,

> Where were you when I laid the earth's foundation?
>> Tell me, if you understand.
> Who marked off its dimensions? Surely you know!

We find ourselves humbled by this sublime passage.

Then come the wonderful stories of the New Testament.

Not only did Jesus speak authoritatively on the deepest is-sues of the human heart, he knew where the fish were biting. In Luke 5:4-11, for instance, Simon and other fishermen came in empty-handed, and Jesus told them to "put out into deep water, and let down the nets." Skeptical but will-ing, they complied, and "they caught such a large number of fish that their nets began to break."

Jesus also knew how to cook fish, no small skill. John 21 describes him grilling fish for his friends over a fire, and Matthew 14:13-21 is one of several accounts where he feeds thousands of people with a few fish and scraps of bread. Anyone who has ever been in charge of a fish fry will appreciate this!

Interested in boats? Jesus spent plenty of time in them, even preached from one (Luke 5:1-4). Fantasized about liv-ing off the land? John the Baptist was a master survivalist (Matthew 3:4). Ever been caught on a lake in rough water? So have the apostles (Mark 4:37-41). Peter even learned, briefly, to walk on water during rough conditions (Matthew 14:22-33). Tempted to brag about your adventures? Better check out Paul's account in 2 Corinthians 11:24-27 first. A partial list includes three shipwrecks, "danger from rivers, in danger from bandits, in danger from my own countrymen, in danger from Gentiles; in danger in the city, in danger in the country, in danger at sea." He even got bitten by a snake when gathering firewood (Acts 28:1-5).

The stories go on and on. Jesus and his buddies were outdoorsmen, not scholars or psychotherapists. They would have been more at home in a flatbottom boat running trotlines than at an academic conference or in a fancy cathedral. When Jesus needed time alone, he headed for the wilderness (Mark 6:46; Luke 9:28), just like a lot of us do.

In case we somehow miss the Bible's emphasis on the outdoors, it concludes in Revelation 21—22 with a description of the finest outdoor destination we can imagine: "a new heaven and a new earth"—better than a Colorado backpacking trek or an Ontario fishing trip. Just as a river flowed from Eden, so will one run through the new heaven and earth: "Then the angel showed me the river of the water of life, as clear as crystal, flowing from the throne of God and of the Lamb," says Revelation 22:1. These divine outdoor experiences don't have to remain a product of the printed page, a realm only of the reader's imagination. After describing the crystal-clear river, Revelation 22:17 says, "Whoever is thirsty, let him come; and whoever wishes, let him take the free gift of the water of life."

I

THE VINEYARD

There's something immensely calming about a vineyard. Whether growing muscadine or Concord grapes, a vineyard has a lush feel, a blend of tangly wild and tamely domestic. It seems the embodiment of nature's goodness.

At least until rattlesnakes enter the picture.

I live in the country, in the woods actually, and snake sightings aren't uncommon. But when some local folks saw twenty-four baby rattlesnakes in one batch, that got my attention.

J. C. and his kinfolk were clearing brush when they noticed rats darting out from a pile. Then a baby snake emerged. Closer inspection revealed a den, and little reptiles began slithering out one and two at a time. The people found the mother under the brush pile and killed her with a stick. She measured four feet, nine inches long. The twenty-four babies were thirteen inches long.

J. C. told me about the experience on a Sunday, and while I thought it was an interesting story, I wasn't personally concerned, since he lives several miles away. The next evening, though, Angelyn and I were outside admiring the flowers beside the driveway when suddenly she jumped and shouted, "A baby snake!"

I chuckled at her alarm, then grew alarmed myself when I saw the eight- to nine-inch serpent leaping and thrashing. After getting a closer look, I smashed it under my boot. It was a baby rattlesnake.

It didn't take a mathematician to reach some disturbing conclusions: J. C. found twenty-four babies; I found one. Where were its littermates? Where was its mama?

I later encountered one of the apparent siblings in my vineyard. I was mowing when I spotted it in the grass. I dispatched it with the lawnmower, feeling grateful I hadn't stepped on it while strolling blissfully among the grapevines. The experience reminded me that for all their Eden-like serenity, vineyards are still part of a fallen world.

In my vineyard, yellowjackets, wasps, bees and hornets buzz about. Ticks and redbugs lurk in the grass. Fire ants build colonies and patrol the ground around them. Mosquitoes carry West Nile virus.

In addition to the dangers inherent in them, vineyards take a good bit of work: mowing, watering, pruning, protecting from predators, insects and diseases. An untended vineyard soon becomes a thicket, the fruit shriveling away to nothing.

But despite all that, when you stand in a well-kept vineyard, immersed in a sea of rambling green studded with grapes, you feel like this is the best that human effort and God-given abundance can provide. Maybe that's why Jesus chose a vineyard as the central image in his speech to the disciples in John 15: "I am the vine; you are the branches."

My vineyard has a rustic cedar bench with two seats and a table in the middle that family members gave me for Christmas. The bench sits in the evening shade of a tulip magnolia tree and looks out across a small, oval lawn surrounded by woods. Posts of pressure-treated lumber with metal spreader arms and wires support half a dozen muscadine vines.

My vines rise four to five feet to the double trellis wires

and extend to the posts on either side, producing a mix of black and bronze grapes. They yield a passable harvest, but deer inflict havoc on them. One year I had a beautiful crop of purple-black grapes dangling from the vines, ready to be picked. I examined them on a weekday and decided Saturday would be the perfect time to gather them. Come Saturday not a single grape remained. I figured the deer did it, since they visit regularly. Actually, they don't visit—they live here. Deer strip leaves off my okra plants, nip my tomato blossoms, rake their horns on the trunks of my fruit trees and leave teeth marks in my Japanese persimmons to test for ripeness.

Before the deer polished off my grape harvest, I had learned that hanging chunks of Ivory soap around fruit trees deters them—whether due to the brightness or scent I can't say—but I hadn't realized my grapevines would need soap too. The next season I cut bars of Ivory in half, notched them, wrapped twine around them and hung them at intervals along the vines. The strategy worked pretty well, but I left the soap hanging out there all year, and apparently the deer grew accustomed to it, because they started nibbling the following year's crop as soon as it appeared. I harvested as soon as the grapes ripened, rather than waiting for an ideal weekend, and thus got to enjoy at least part of the bounty. My next strategy will be strips of cloth doused with after-shave lotion, which I'm told is effective. Yet I worry that raccoons, not deer, may also be involved—what do I do about them?

The situation reminds me of the story Jesus begins in Matthew 21:33 when he says, "There was a landowner who planted a vineyard. He put a wall around it . . . and built a watchtower." That's what I need: a wall and a watchtower.

To the left of the cedar bench in my vineyard stands a massive fig tree. The tree was tall when we got ready to build our current house in 1990; problem was, it was standing on the proposed house site. Angelyn wanted to transplant it, but I assured her a tree that size would never survive. With the determination of a true plant lover, she enlisted our son Andy, and they dug up and moved the tree to its present spot despite my scoffing. The tree flourished.

The limbs now sprawl to thirty feet in diameter, creating a rounded green universe. I fertilize it regularly with kitchen scraps—eggshells, banana peels, onion skins, coffee grounds—which I cover with dirt to keep down smells and bugs. The tree pays us back in abundance every July. We eat our fill of figs, share with neighbors and have plenty left over for the birds. In fact, I leave the high upper tier of fruit just for them since it's so hard to get to anyway. We don't make preserves, just eat the fruit fresh, but sometimes a recipient, like a fellow church member, makes a batch and gives us some.

There are other delights visible from my vineyard bench as well: a couple of raised beds where I grow tomatoes, okra, peppers and squash, bordered by purple gomphrena flowers; a row of quince trees; various ornamental plants like roses, hibiscus, weeping crepe myrtle and white azaleas; and sprawling ferns at the edge of the woods.

In the Bible, lush gardens and fruitful vines are symbols of peace and well-being. "During Solomon's lifetime Judah and Israel, from Dan to Beersheba, lived in safety, each man under his own vine and fig tree," records 1 Kings 4:25.

The prophet Micah, in chapter 4 of his namesake book, describes a blissful future when

> they will beat their swords into plowshares
> > and their spears into pruning hooks.
> Nation will not take up sword against nation,

nor will they train for war anymore.
Every man will sit under his own vine
    and under his own fig tree,
and no one will make them afraid,
    for the LORD Almighty has spoken.

But those days aren't here yet, as snakes and bugs, wars and terrorist attacks graphically remind us—and the Bible long ago warned us. "While people are saying, 'Peace and safety,' destruction will come on them suddenly," predicted the apostle Paul in I Thessalonians 5:3.

I love the serenity of my vineyard, but I'm not fooled. As fine as it is, it's just a dim reflection of the true vineyard I hope to enjoy someday.

2

THE KINGDOM OF HEAVEN

I'm not normally comfortable handling babies. I'm so big, and they're so small. But when my son handed me my first-ever grandbaby in December 1998 when I was forty-three years old, I didn't feel the slightest discomfort. She fit exactly in my arms. Since then I've held Ella Martin Coy every chance I've had, sometimes competing with my wife for the privilege.

I'm not often bowled over by babies. When someone brings an infant into the newspaper office where I work, I'm rarely among the crowd of cooers and gushers. But Ella reminded me that there's nothing more extraordinary than a baby.

Consider her hair, for example. It's red, like her mother's. It glows around her head like live embers spun into silk. And her face. At one moment I see traits of her maternal grandfather, in another that of my son Andy, while a third glance shows no one but Ella herself.

Is it any wonder Jesus doted on children? He who saw to the heart of things easily recognized their semi-divine quality. "Then little children were brought to Jesus for him to place his hands on them and pray for them. But the disciples rebuked those who brought them.

"Jesus said, 'Let the little children come to me, and do not hinder them, for the kingdom of heaven belongs to such as these,' " says Matthew 19:13-14.

Over the ensuing years, Ella has been giving me a variety of glimpses into that kingdom, such as the time when she was two and a half and we sat in the grass and ate wild strawberries together. Normally such berries are beneath my notice. They're bland, small and common as weeds. But with Ella around, my perspective changes.

Since Andy and Paulette live seven hours away, Angelyn and I only get to see Ella every couple months or so. As a result, we catch her in a different stage of development each time. During this visit, she was a walking, talking bundle of curiosity. Everything interested her: a flower, a bug, a lizard—if it existed, it was worthy of her attention, especially if it was outdoors. She's an outdoors girl. And this particular day was an outdoors day.

We started on the front porch and worked gradually outward. Pet the cats. Water the plants. Walk in the grass. Listen to the birds. Sniff the flowers. In the orchard Ella saw some blueberry bushes loaded with unripe fruit. We told her they'd be sour, but she had to see for herself. So she plucked one and popped it into her mouth. At first her expression was skeptical, as if to say, "Sour? What sour?" Then she bit down. "Yuck! Nasty!" she declared, spitting dramatically.

I decided the remedy was some ripe huckleberries, so we trekked over to a bush where I'd seen some recently. Angelyn and I showed Ella how to identify and pick the ripe ones. We squatted in the grass eating the BB-sized, purple-black berries, which are also normally beneath my notice. This day, though, they were exquisite. The bush itself was a thing of beauty, my wife pointed out, particularly when you crouch under it and peer up through the mass of small green leaves to the blue sky. Funny we'd never noticed that before.

As we continued our circuit we came upon a prime patch of wild strawberries. There was nothing to do but stop and dine. I sat cross-legged with Ella in my lap, and Angelyn kept us supplied with fruit. We studied the berries' bright red color, then popped them into our mouths and felt their subtle flavor unfold on our tongues, their quiet crunchiness on our teeth.

A year later, when Ella was three and a half, we decided to get more adventurous and introduce her to canoeing. For the afternoon jaunt Angelyn packed as much gear as I normally take on a weekend camping trip: toys, snacks, drinks, towels, sunscreen, bug spray, headgear, footwear and I don't know what else. As we drove up to the local state park lake, Ella pointed and said, "Crocodiles!" I assured her there were no crocodiles here as I tried to put a child-sized life vest on her. It was too small, so I used a small adult vest, which swallowed her up like an astronaut suit. I strapped it into place with a bungee cord, and Angelyn pulled a tightly cinched, adult-sized camouflage cap over Ella's red hair. I held the canoe steady while Angelyn got in, then hoisted Ella onto a boat cushion in front of her. I took my seat in the stern, and we were off.

As we headed out onto the open lake, I asked for a status report. Angelyn said things were looking "s-c-a-r-y." We agreed to stick close to shore to minimize terror, but looming clumps of swamp grass brought squeaks of fear, so I hustled us back toward the main lake.

"Ella said she's ready to go back," Angelyn announced.

We had been out five minutes.

"OK, we'll just make a big circle," I said.

Forget my plan to go up the river and explore its backwaters. I pointed us directly across the lake.

"Legs!" Ella wailed.

"It's just a granddaddy longlegs, honey," Angelyn told her.

Ella's seat was so low that her main view was the inside of the boat, including the dark crevice in the bow where insects lurked. Also limiting her visibility was the life vest that came up around her ears and the cap that came down to her eyes. The giant vest also restricted her movement and blocked the occasional breeze.

To brighten her mood, I eased up to a patch of weeds where colorful purple flowers grew. We picked one and Ella did seem thrilled, relatively. A visiting dragonfly or two also helped distract her. We made a brief detour along the bank, then turned back toward the home shore. With the truck coming into sight, Ella began to relax.

I propelled us slowly, wanting to make this last as long as I could. We approached a white egret and a great blue heron standing in shallows mid-lake. They flew, providing momentary diversion. We paused in a patch of lily pads to pick a yellow flower.

When we reached shore, I realized what an accomplishment it was: Ella's first canoe trip! We applauded her and told her what a great job she'd done. As she posed for a photo, our little red-headed adventurer beamed proudly, flower in hand.

"I tell you the truth," Jesus says in Mark 10:15, "anyone who will not receive the kingdom of God like a little child will never enter it."

When Ella pauses to taste the wonder in a wild strawberry, gazes heavenward through a graceful network of huckleberry branches or overcomes her fears to pick a colorful swamp lily, she helps me understand what he means.

A LONELY PLACE

Used to be my wilderness role models were mountain men and jungle explorers. But when I took a solitary float-camping trip down the upper Pearl River of central Mississippi, I thought not of Jeremiah Johnson or H. M. Stanley but of Jesus.

"He went up on a mountainside by himself to pray," says Matthew 14:23.

"One of those days Jesus went out to a mountainside to pray, and spent the night praying to God," says Luke 6:12.

"But Jesus often withdrew to lonely places and prayed," notes Luke 5:16.

Those verses leave out a lot of details. The desert is hot

in the daytime, cold at night and bereft of drinking water. Did Jesus take food? a canteen? a blanket? We don't know. The impression is that he just walked up the side of a mountain, knelt down and prayed. But try setting out on an overnight trek into a "lonely place" and see if you don't take something with you.

As I packed for my twenty-mile float, I first considered taking only a coat, sleeping bag, canteen, maybe some bread. But I remembered my youthful forays into the woods when I tried to rough it and wound up cold, wet and hungry. So I went ahead and packed my usual gear: tent, sleeping bag and pad, camp stove, utensils, extra clothes and various accessories.

I parked my truck at the takeout, a lowhead dam, and a friend dropped me and my boat off at the put-in, a rural bridge. My idea was to drift, meditate and pray, rather like Jesus did. Of course, the upper Pearl River is far removed from the wilderness of Judea. It's a shallow, logjammed creek for miles, then widens as it approaches Ross Barnett Reservoir. I thought surely it would be big enough for easy floating, and I set out in high spirits, my prayers wafting to the blue sky amid a swirl of autumn leaves.

I enumerated my blessings and thanked God for them,

asked him to take care of each of my loved ones, prayed for everybody from county officials to world leaders, revisited problems and experiences I had recently undergone. Then came a logjam. Downed trees stretched clear across the river, and I had to drag the boat over them. Next were sandy shallows. I had to get out and tow. More logs. More shoals. Before long I was muttering, "Not again!" "Oh, come on!" After a while I realized I wasn't exactly imitating the Savior.

But hiking in the desert mountains probably wasn't so easy either. The ground is rough and rocky, the plants thorny, and Jesus was wearing sandals. I pictured him heading uphill and encountering a series of steep ravines, forcing him either to clamber across or detour around. Did he gripe and whine?

I don't think so.

So I calmed down and tried to resume my praying.

For me, such prayers are as free flowing as a river. Sometimes they take the form of specific thoughts, but other times they're just a sense of openness to God. After I had prayed for every specific subject I could think of, I unlatched my mind and let God's Spirit sift in like sunlight through pine boughs.

By dusk the river had widened. But now there was a new

problem: no sandbars to camp on. As I passed under a bridge, I saw nothing but a long, wide sheet of water between high, steep banks topped with jungly thickets. Not even a hint of a camping spot. I would have to keep paddling in the dark.

As I ate a quick supper of cheese and crackers, I thought of alligators, which are legendary on Ross Barnett Reservoir and the Pearl River—big gators too, some of them longer than my fourteen-foot canoe.

In Jesus' day the desert was home to wolves, jackals, snakes, maybe mountain lions. Did he take a weapon? A sword, a spear or even a staff? A staff, maybe. But I suspect the wild animals would know instinctively that he was the Son of God. Being purely mortal, I strapped on a .22-caliber pistol, stuck a flashlight in my pocket and resumed paddling.

The daylight faded, and the moon wasn't enough to light my way. I dodged some limbs and found myself beached in the shallows. Then I noticed a sandbar, silver in the moonlight. So I made camp. Pitched a tent. Sat down and lit a cigar.

Of course, there was no tobacco in Jesus' day, at least not in the Middle East. And even if there had been, I can't see him puffing a stogie while he prayed on the mountainside. But I found it soothing as I sat in the moonlight listening to the sounds of the night: distant highway traffic, the put-tering four-wheelers of raccoon hunters and the occasional bay of hounds.

After I turned in, the wind picked up, clouds curtained the moon, and rain swept against the tent. Did it ever rain on Jesus when he "withdrew to lonely places"? Would he have cared? The Bible said he suffered the travails of mortal flesh, and a night rain can chill you to the bone. Dry and cozy in my tent, I zipped my sleeping bag up tight and was glad for my gear.

The misty dawn to which I awoke was conducive to prayer. I praised God for these incredibly beautiful woods, haunting in the morning fog. Yet I soon confronted another problem: this stretch of river had no current; it was backed up and slack as it approached the reservoir. Propelled only by my paddle, I moved at a crawl.

Gradually, my prayerful mood evaporated. It was taking forever to get to the takeout. Bend after currentless bend greeted me. The wrist I broke earlier in the year throbbed like a toothache.

Did Jesus suffer aches and pains on his treks? If so, I'm sure he didn't whine about them. I tried to relax.

Finally I arrived at the takeout and loaded my boat and

gear into my pickup truck. I had come down from the mountain.

In many ways I had failed to measure up to my role model. I wasn't tough enough or brave enough to leave behind my food and gear. I carried a weapon. I griped about petty obstacles. Yet I felt like I had accomplished something anyway. I had done a lot of praying and reflecting, and I had genuinely tried to imitate the Savior. I'm not Jesus, just one of his followers. But in my own insignificant way, I too "withdrew to lonely places and prayed."

4

WOODS FULL OF TREASURE

One drawback to living in an affluent society is that we have forgotten about many of the gifts nature has to offer—gifts that people like Daniel Boone were well familiar with. It astounds me, for instance, how few people nowadays know what a pawpaw is, though I'll admit that for years I didn't know either.

I discovered the luscious fruit in the Arkansas woods on a canoe trip. But I didn't realize we had them in southwest Mississippi where I live until I chanced across some while picking the wild grapes known as muscadines. I had been monitoring the status of muscadines for several weeks and figured they would be ripe by Labor Day. So when the day came, I set out for the creek with buckets and fishing tackle. I walked a mile through the woods to intersect it, planning to wade back upstream to my truck. I would fish each stretch first, then hunt for muscadines.

For over an hour I found neither fish nor fruit. My luck began to change when I hooked a bass too small to keep but exciting anyway. Then I found a grapevine of biblical proportions. It was draped over a tree far above the creek, loaded down with black muscadines. The fruit looked as unreachable as the Amorite vineyards seemed to the Israelites in Deuteronomy I. Moses' spies found a land of abundance but were afraid to challenge the inhabitants. I wasn't afraid; I just couldn't get to those grapes. When I shook the vines, the muscadines plunked into the water and quickly rolled away in the swift current. I considered climbing the tree, but the fruit was far out of reach. So, like the faithless Israelites, I gave up and resumed my wanderings in the wilderness.

As with the Israelites, God gave me another chance: I caught another bass. This one was big enough to keep, but I released it anyway. Then I noticed a heavily loaded vine over a sandbar, the best place to collect wild muscadines. When you shake the vine or throw sticks at it, the grapes fall onto the sand and you can pick them up. Some folks even spread bed sheets on the ground.

Looking around for a good throwing stick, I wandered up into the woods. The slender trees growing all around looked mighty familiar. Then I recognized them: pawpaws! I had found the promised land. Not milk and honey, maybe, but muscadines and pawpaws.

A pawpaw resembles a cross between a pear and a persimmon—oblong and mottled green with creamy yellow fruit and big seeds, and leaves that look like hickory. To eat them, you just break them open and bite. They taste like vanilla pudding—delicious and oh so sweet. Pawpaws are harvested by first picking the ones within reach and then shaking the trunks for the rest, taking care they don't bonk you on the head. In no time you can collect all you can eat. But there's no point in gathering too many because, like Old Testament manna, pawpaws are notoriously perishable, one reason they haven't become a big commercial crop.

Loaded with pawpaws, I returned to my muscadine vine, where I threw sticks into it to make the muscadines rain down. While I bent down to get them, sky-blue flowers winked up at me through the grass, reminding me that God provides pleasures for the eye as well as the palate.

Continuing upstream, I surprised a squirrel in a tree. The startled creature fell off its limb and tumbled ten feet to the water. It came up sputtering, dashed to the trunk and peeked around at me, then whisked up the tree.

Later I came to a swift bend in the river with an adjacent backwater. By my calculations a bass should be hanging right at the eddy's edge waiting for something to eat. No sooner did my lure hit the water than *wham!* The hooked largemouth raced into the eddy, so I was fighting current as well as fish. I wrestled him in, a brawling one-pounder, decent-sized for a creek bass. Feeling charitable, I released him as well.

All the while the sweet September breeze jostled the cricket-humming woods, birds danced among the trees, and the river swirled cold around my pant legs. Wild and free with such delights, I couldn't help but get the feeling that God's in his heaven and all is right with the world.

Unlike me, frontiersmen and women hunted, fished and gathered not for recreation but for sustenance. They could teach us a lot about living off the land, and about other things as well. That became clear to me when I came across an intriguing quote by Daniel Boone.

Most people know that Boone was a master woodsman,

of course, but history-minded people may also be aware that he was a Revolutionary War soldier and later in life, a state legislator. Still, probably few think of him as a theologian. Okay, maybe that's too strong a word, but a statement by Boone sums up the Christian philosophy as succinctly as any I have seen outside the Bible: "The religion I have is to love and fear God, believe in Jesus Christ, do all the good to my neighbor and myself that I can, do as little harm as I can help, and trust on God's mercy for the rest."

There's something to be said for the lessons learned in the woods—whether finding food or discerning God—in contrast to those derived from textbooks and commentaries. Romans 1:20 says straight out, "For since the creation of the world God's invisible qualities—his eternal power and divine nature—have been clearly seen, being understood from what has been made." Life in the woods tends to hone theological issues down to a fine edge, like a whetstone applied to a skinning knife.

We don't have to have all the answers, or even most of them. What we need is simple faith and love for others. It's fitting that such wisdom was summed up in simple terms by a rustic backwoodsman.

5

CROWN OF THORNS

When my pastor asked me to get some thorns for a church Easter exhibit, I had no idea it would involve getting lost in the swamp. I figured I'd just walk out in the woods one day and cut a sawbriar vine—though I had to admit sawbriar thorns are short and wouldn't be highly visible on the wooden cross outside our little country church. The thorns, of course, would be used to create a replica of the crown Jesus wore when he was crucified.

Meanwhile, when my pal Eddie McCalip and I set out to go canoeing in Louisiana, I was thinking about weather, not church projects. The forecast called for a 100-percent chance of rain, with flash floods across Louisiana and Mississippi. Not a good time to go canoeing, I admit. But I was particularly determined since I was writing a canoeing guide to Louisiana at the time.

At first we planned to float Boeuf River in east-central Louisiana, but it was already at flood stage, so we decided to take our chances with the northwest part of the state instead. When we pulled up at the old bridge at Dixie Inn, Bayou Dorcheat was nipping dangerously at the underside of the concrete. We drove on to safer waters at Bayou Bodcau below the dam at Bodcau Wildlife Management Area. There, though the water was high the dam slowed the current considerably. But my optimism faltered when, on the cassette player in my truck, Ralph Stanley and the Clinch Mountain Boys wailed the haunting lament "Oh, Death."

We parked my truck at the Highway 157 bridge, drove back to the dam-side campground in Eddie's Jeep and launched our canoes. Four miles of bayou paddling should take a couple of hours. It was 1:30 p.m., so we had plenty of time.

The bayou was white with foam from the churning action of the spillway. But it soon slowed as it passed between cypress woods swaddled in cottony Spanish moss. Eddie, whose jobs include producing a TV nature show, took advantage of a lull in the rain to film this rare beauty. Then we rounded a bend, and Bodcau spread out into the woods with no discernible channel. I'd visited this bayou a few weeks previously and discovered its tricky nature. But that was when water levels were normal.

**"Rising water levels heighten concerns:
More rain, flooding is forecast for the area."**

"Homeowners are sandbagging, cattle are moving to higher ground, and the waters just keep rising."

"Officials work to shore up low-lying areas."

"High water halts barge navigation on Red River."

—from the *Times of Shreveport*

As we picked a route through the woods in a southerly direction, rain began to peck the dark water. Nothing but trackless swamp spread in all directions, and there was no sign of the bayou.

It was about then that I saw a perfect thornbush rising out of the water. Unlike sawbriars, these thorns were one to two inches long. I pulled out my Swiss Army knife, glad to have found a practical use for the saw blade. Soon two long thorny branches lay in the bottom of the canoe.

"So you think this is ordained?" Eddie asked me when I told him about my pastor's request.

"Why, certainly," I said. But if God had sent us off course to lead me to a crown of thorns, he wasn't through with us yet.

When we emerged onto a channel again, it took us nowhere. In fact, each time we found what appeared to be the bayou, it dead-ended in dense brush or high ground. Too bad I didn't have a global positioning system (GPS) or quadrangle map since I had merely glanced at a topographic atlas before setting out.

Finally, with the rain picking up, the temperature falling and the daylight fading, I had to admit that I didn't have a clue where the bayou was. I felt a twinge of panic. During thirty years of adventuring in remote places I had encountered worse situations, but that wasn't solving our problem now. This was early March, hypothermia weather, and it looked like we might have to spend the night out here. All I had for protection was a jean jacket and a poncho, both damp. I envisioned shivering the night away in the boat or struggling to build a fire on shore with waterlogged wood.

Then I looked down at the thorns, which put my fears into perspective.

Then the governor's soldiers took Jesus into the Praetorium and gathered the whole company of soldiers around him. They stripped him and put a scarlet robe on him, and then twisted together a crown of thorns and set it on his head. They put a staff in his right hand and knelt in front of him and mocked him. "Hail, king of the Jews!" they said. They spit on him, and took the staff and struck him on the head again and again. After they had mocked him, they took off the robe and put his own clothes on him. Then they led him away to crucify him. (Matthew 27:27-31)

Eddie and I decided to try to walk out. We spotted some high ground and set out into the woods on foot. We found a deer ladder stand, and from its perch I took a compass bearing on a distant clearing. We located my truck about a mile and a half away. It was 5:30 p.m., not quite dark. Prayer answered.

We drove to the campground and holed up in our tents.

As rain continued to fall and the temperature dropped into the forties, I thanked God we weren't having to bivouac in the swamp.

Our task in the morning was to hike back in, locate our canoes, then find our way to the bridge. As I got into my truck and pushed in the Ralph Stanley tape, the first song I heard was "Jesus Savior, Pilot Me."

We left my truck at the bridge, parked Eddie's Jeep at the spot we had emerged from the woods, hiked back to the boats, bailed out the rainwater and started paddling. This time we knew which direction to go. Plus I had a machete in case brush blocked our our way. But the going was easy. Rain tapped gently down as we cruised through the flooded forest. In an hour's time we were at the bridge, loading our boats onto our vehicles.

We broke camp, ate lunch in town, and as I hit Interstate 20 I pushed the tape in. "Traveling the highway home," the Clinch Mountain Boys sang.

I handed the thorns to my pastor at church the next morning.

6

BLUEGRASS GOSPEL

There are few sounds purer than bluegrass instruments ringing out from the front porch of a deep-woods cabin, like the one I visited one cool, sunny day in southwest Mississippi. Members of a bluegrass group called McCall Creek built the retreat deep in the piney woods. They cut trees on the property and hired a portable sawmill operator to cut the wood into planks, then planed the boards themselves. The result was a twenty-by-twenty-foot structure with a twelve-by-twenty-foot room, an eight-foot-deep porch, a small back stoop and a tin roof.

Inside were a small wooden table made with square nails, ceramic pitchers and basins, lanterns, a pie safe, a glider, a chifforobe, leather-bottomed chairs, rustic beds, a split-log bench, a large old Prince Albert can, a chamber pot, a lap harp, a wagon wheel chandelier and assorted baskets. On the wall hung a photo of group member Linda Spring's grandfather sitting barefoot on a front porch wearing overalls, holding a single-barrel shotgun and laughing. Linda still has her grandfather's fiddle.

I joined Linda and fellow McCall Creek member Hank Howell on the front porch for some picking. A black dog snoozed out front, smoke rose from an outdoor fire, and the creek chimed down below. While I played claw hammer banjo and Linda plucked a mandolin, Hank strummed the guitar and sang tunes like "Arkansas," "I'm So Lonesome I Could Cry," "Those Memories," "Wildflowers Don't Care Where They Grow," "I Cried Again," "Angel Band," "Love of the Mountain" and "Unclouded Day." Gospel, country and bluegrass mingle easily here in the Deep South.

Musicians like Hank and Linda are carrying on a very old tradition. In the Old Testament, King David "told the leaders of the Levites to appoint their brothers as singers to sing joyful songs, accompanied by musical instruments: lyres, harps and cymbals," says I Chronicles 15:16. The chapter even lists the musicians. Thousands of years later, we can still read their names.

Nowadays the most publicity many gospel musicians are likely to receive is inclusion in a church bulletin, considerably more ephemeral than the Old Testament. The income, if any, may be from sales of the occasional self-produced compact disk or cassette tape. Yet gospel music is a vital ministry. It may not produce mass conversions or miraculous healings, but it vibrates the heartstrings just as it did in David's time.

My own route to gospel music was probably typical. As a teenaged guitarist I played folk, rock and blues. One day at an outdoor craft fair in Memphis, Tennessee, I was mesmerized by the sounds of fiddle, dulcimer, guitar and banjo—a bluegrass band playing "Bonaparte's Retreat." I've never forgotten the way that music stirred my blood.

I plinked around on fiddle, mandolin and banjo off and on after that, and wound up sticking with the banjo. Maybe it's a descendant of those lyres and harps in King David's court. While it is occasionally employed for corny music ("Raindrops Keep Falling on My Head," "Love Me Tender"), it can also reach heights of haunting beauty, like the splash of water in a mountain glen. It, along with other traditional instruments—dobro, guitar, fiddle, mandolin, dulcimer, string bass, even harmonica at times—is perfect for songs like "Build Me a Cabin in the Corner of Gloryland," "Precious Memories" and "I'll Fly Away."

Bluegrass gospel airs on local, state and nationally syndicated radio shows nowadays. But people who only hear it on radio, television or stereo may not realize that it's essentially an outdoor music style. Bluegrass festivals are traditionally held outdoors, like the hoedowns on the courthouse square each spring and fall in a small town near my house. My wife says my banjo sounds better on the front porch, where it rings out through the surrounding woods, than in the confines of the house. She likes me to play it while she's working in the yard; our cats seem to enjoy it too, judging by the way they gather around, sometimes jumping up and sniffing the strings.

I often take instruments with me when I go camping. My fiddle has accompanied the splashing of an eighteen-foot waterfall in the rugged Tunica Hills near the Mississippi River. A crackling campfire played percussion as I plucked the banjo by Louisiana's sleepy Tchefuncte River; owls gathered around camp when I blew my harmonica on nearby Tangipahoa River. A guitar eased my summertime blues on a scorching canoe trip down Arkansas's Ouachita River, and my banjolin—a cross between a banjo and a mandolin—rang out at Lower Kintla Lake in Montana's Glacier National Park beneath ten-thousand-foot mountains.

These instruments sound better in the outdoors than in buildings, with one exception—the church house. Whether it's due to the acoustics of a church sanctuary or the spirit of the place, bluegrass instruments really resonate there.

Every first Monday night of the month, various musicians meet at my own church, Woodland United Methodist, to play bluegrass, gospel and country. These musicians have come from various denominations, including Methodist, Baptist, Full Gospel, Assembly of God, Church of Christ—there's even been a nonbeliever or two.

One day a friend named Callie Chapman heard me play "Sweet By and By" on the banjo and asked if we'd perform at her church. I relayed the request to my fellow musicians, who shrugged and said sure. That's how our white bluegrass gospel group came to play at Beulah Land Church of God in Christ, a black Pentecostal church.

The Beulah Land church occasion was both homecoming and fundraiser. Members were trying to raise money to replace a termite-damaged floor. With a large crowd expected, the service was held at Embry Hill Church a few miles to the west, way out in the country. We arrived at Embry Hill shortly before the one p.m. Sunday service, strolled past the big shady oaks and went inside, where we tuned our instruments and took our place in the sanctuary.

The Church of God in Christ denomination was founded in 1897 with an emphasis on sanctification—becoming holy—and speaking in tongues. It was part of a Pentecostal movement that swept the nation. Beulah Land members describe their church as a "foot-stomping, hand-clapping church."

Though the service had a program, Superintendent Odell Franklin, Beulah Land pastor, noted, "We don't try to program God." He kicked off the service with a rhythmic prayer to the background music of a bass guitar and keyboards and members of the audience chiming in. More songs followed, along with testimony and even a spontaneous dance by an eighty-year-old woman celebrating her birthday. If I can do this at eighty, she challenged us, what can you do in your twenties, thirties and forties?

Our music was a bit different, but the audience still clapped in time as we played "Unclouded Day," "Sweet By and By" and "Where Could I Go?" with fiddle, dobro, two guitars, a singer and my banjo. I didn't make any speeches, but if I had, I would have pointed out that since the banjo is of African origin with Scottish American modifications, it combines the ingenuity of both Africans and Caucasians and has been used for styles ranging from blues to bluegrass.

After we played, we settled in for the sermon. The preacher's wide-ranging message concluded with some comments on race—significant considering that immediately behind him sat two white pastors who were members of our group. He noted that not many decades ago, the sight of blacks and whites worshiping together in Mississippi was not only rare but possibly dangerous, and he credited the changing hearts to the Holy Spirit. Following his sermon, he embraced both white pastors on the podium.

People from all over observed the moment, including members from several sister churches, plus former Beulah Land members visiting from Chicago, New Orleans and elsewhere, not to mention us bluegrass folks. It was one more proof that gospel music has a way of bringing people together, whether on the front porch of a country cabin, in King David's court, deep in the wilderness or at an interracial church service in Mississippi.

7

ROUGH SEAS

Those of us who are landlubbers often breeze through New Testament passages of stormy waters without much empathy. Those silly old apostles were always getting into rough conditions in the Sea of Galilee, then crying out to the Lord to save them, right?

But it's instructive to set out into saltwater now and then, just for perspective into what their experiences as sailors were like.

In Jesus' day, boats were built differently than they are today. Builders used a "shell first" construction, assembling the hull first and inserting the frames later. The more modern "skeleton first" method is to build the frame, then add the planking. In Bible times the Sea of Galilee abounded with hundreds of fishing boats. That "sea," also known as Lake Gennesaret, is a mere 7.5 by 13 miles. It is the major water supply for the nation of Israel, and a dam now stands at its lower end.

In 1985 a couple of Israeli fishermen were walking the mud flats around the Sea of Galilee looking for artifacts when they found the remains of an old boat—a really old boat. Water levels were down due to a drought, and a Jeep had gouged ruts in the flats, revealing old bits of wood. The men, who were brothers, called the officials, and government archaeologist Shelley Wachsmann appeared on the scene. It took a massive effort to raise the twenty-seven-foot-long husk from the mud as archaeologists faced seeping ground water and rising lake levels, Wachsmann writes in his book *The Sea of Galilee Boat: An Extraordinary 2000-Year-Old Discovery*. Eventually, however, they got the vessel up and began the search for a museum.

The Sea of Galilee boat was one foot longer than the sailboat Scott and I used to check out the Mississippi Sound, the portion of the Gulf of Mexico between the Mississippi coast and a line of barrier islands several miles offshore. We launched from a marina in six-mile-wide Bay St. Louis—

about the width of the Sea of Galilee. To get to sailing waters, we would have to pass under a drawbridge, follow a narrow, marked channel for nearly three miles, then go through two more drawbridges, one at a highway and the next at a railroad, and out to the Mississippi Sound.

Since I'm prone to motion sickness, I pretty much avoid the sea, but when a good friend invites you out on his new sailboat, what can you do? I downed a seasickness pill and off we went, propelled by a 9.9-horsepower, four-stroke motor.

The first drawbridge was a slow mover, rising from one end rather than in the middle. A tail wind was shoving us pretty fast, and we had a tense moment as we approached the rusty bridge before it was fully up. We skimmed under, our eyes on the mast top. Scott has sea-kayaked all over creation and built various wooden boats, but this was his first real sailboat (not counting a small catamaran). Despite his many miles on saltwater, he admitted he had much to learn about single-handing.

He gave me the tiller and I tried to keep us in the narrow channel. Most of the bay is just three to five feet deep, not enough for a bluewater hull, which may draw four feet or more. Veer a bit to either side of the channel and the depth-finder went from seven feet to five or less in a hurry. It was strange to stare at the expanse of open water and realize it was too shallow to sail, at least for us. I felt for those ancient mariners like the apostles, who had no depth-finders, markers or charts.

The bay grew choppy as we pointed the sleek bow toward the next drawbridge. Scott radioed the operator, who opened it promptly. At the railroad drawbridge a train was coming, so we spent a miserable thirty minutes in the wind-whipped slot between the two bridges, motoring in circles. My motion sickness pill wasn't enough to ward off waves of dizziness before the creaky old trestle swung sideways and let us through.

We emerged into the Mississippi Sound, with broad, choppy reaches of water eight to ten feet deep. Scott told me to keep the bow into the wind while he raised sail. He clipped his safety harness on and scampered on top of the bouncing cabin, wrestling with the triangular mainsail. There was a thud, a scuffle, and he hollered that the boom had fallen off the block, or some such nautical expression. In other words, the bar beneath the sail had come loose from the mast. That's not supposed to happen.

"Grab that orange rope!" he yelled into the wind.

With the wooden tiller in my right hand, I grabbed the

rope with my left despite its being sore from physical therapy for a broken wrist. Meanwhile Scott wrestled with the boom like Marines raising the flag at Iwo Jima.

"I can't get it!" he said after fifteen minutes of commotion.

Great. The boat was falling apart, the waves were throwing us around like a rubber duck in a washing machine, and a train was stopped on the drawbridge behind us so we couldn't retreat even if we tried. As I watched Scott struggle, I prayed, "Lord, give him the strength of an angel."

Another thud. Scott turned. "Got it!" Soon we were sailing. "That's just sailboat stuff," he said, dismissing our near catastrophe.

I wonder if that's anything like the way it was on the night the apostles saw Jesus walking on the water. According to Matthew 14:22-34, they were contending with rough waves when they saw him approach. Peter (who I daresay wasn't bothered by seasickness) wanted to join him, and with Jesus' permission he hopped out of the boat and took a few steps. Then he began to doubt.

Matthew says it was the force of the wind that caused Peter to panic. But I can imagine thoughts that might distract more modern minds: *What if Jesus is just hypnotizing me and I'm not really walking on water? Even if I am walking on water, this is purely an anecdotal incident and not scientifically verifiable or statistically supportable. Besides, there's probably a one in a billion chance that someone could walk on water without supernatural assistance, so this doesn't necessarily prove anything. I'll bet when you factor in the barometric pressure, salinity of the water, force of the wind and pull of the tides, this is easily explainable. . . . My feet are getting wet. . . . What kind of God would let me walk on water while so many others sink? Walking on water doesn't cure any of the world's problems, so what good is it? . . . Hey, now that I'm walking on water, maybe I'm as powerful as Jesus and don't really need him anymore. . . . What if there is some kind of time limit to walking on water, and mine is about to run out? . . . It was warmer in the boat. . . . Who's to say I couldn't walk on water with some other religious leader instead of Jesus, say, Buddha, Muhammad or Shirley MacLaine? . . . Maybe I can write a book about my experience and go on the talk-show circuit. Jesus and I could charge people to watch, donating a percentage of the take to charity, of course. Speaking of spectators, I wonder if any good-looking women are watching me right now. . . . Say, is Jesus going to charge me for this?*

When Peter doubted, he began to sink, and his reaction, naturally, was to yell, "Lord, save me!" Sound familiar?

Jesus reached out and caught him, saying, "You of little faith, why did you doubt?"

Again, I can think of answers a modern mind might come

up with: *It's human nature, Jesus. Look at the ancient Israelites; they were always doubting. Even Moses doubted. Besides, there are two sides to every issue. I was just being open-minded.*

Peter and the other disciples, however, simply said, "Truly you are the Son of God."

Funny, the lessons you can learn at sea.

8

THAT LITTLE
CHURCH HOUSE ON THE HILL

Owls aren't uncommon where I live. In the late evenings sitting on the porch we're liable to hear the eerie, high-pitched whinny of screech owls, the raucous cries of barred owls or the dignified, deep-throated hoots of great horned owls. Occasionally we even see them swooping low through the woods at dusk or lighting on a branch near the house.

But I never expected to find one in church.

Members arrived at our little country church for worship one Sunday morning to find a small screech owl perched on a hanging light fixture. It blinked at us as if we, not it, were the intruders. It remained in place throughout the service, and when I glanced up during the sermon, I noticed it was asleep.

Maybe we shouldn't have been all that surprised. Woodland United Methodist Church is well named, being located in the midst of woods and farmland and less than a mile from a national forest. It's the sort of white-frame country church you see on Christmas cards or envision when you hear songs like "That Little Church House on the Hill." Through the sanctuary windows we've observed deer, wild turkeys, even an emu escaped from a nearby farm. A large red-tailed salamander lives under the front porch step, and snakes inhabit the piles of old lumber under the hundred-year-old building.

We were able to remove the owl with the help of a dip net, and I even wrote a newspaper column about it. I dutifully reported that the owl slept through the sermon, which much amused the preacher, who clipped the column out and laughed about the incident for years.

I remembered that incident one weekday summer afternoon many years later when I went to the church to do a little painting. Dressed in work clothes, I drove up to the old, white-frame church, its steeply pitched green metal roof shaded by big oaks. As I stepped inside, an aura of sanctity enveloped me. First there was the familiar smell of an old wooden building, dimly pungent and sweet. Then there were the rows of empty pews in the darkened sanctuary, the cool blue of the carpet, the warm wood tones of the altar, podium and cross on the wall. Afternoon light filtered through the tall, peaked windows, each of them bordered by blue and yellow stained-glass squares. Through the clear panes I saw the boughs of ancient trees framing a green pasture where cattle lazily grazed. I stood in the hushed room, thinking of all the Sundays I've spent there, of the many other people who have worshiped there, the countless hymns sung, sermons preached, prayers uttered, Sunday schools conducted.

I stepped into the small annex, which serves as the children's Sunday school room, the kitchen and the fellowship hall. How many cups of coffee and pieces of cake have been shared here, stories told, peals of laughter rung out? I found the paint bucket in a cabinet and went outside to stir. The paint was thick, so I stretched out in the shade to take my time. A breeze idled across the pasture and crinkled the oak leaves. How many dinners have been served on the grounds out here, tables laden with chicken pie, homemade pimiento cheese sandwiches, casseroles, vegetables and desserts of every sort?

Sometimes I think churchgoers are most Christian not when we're sitting in church singing hymns or listening to the sermon but when we break bread together, whether that bread is a full meal or just coffee cake. At Woodland we have snacks each Sunday after worship. People rotate bringing goodies, and we pile into the small, sunlit fellowship room for coffee, juice, soft drinks, cookies, cake, doughnuts or cupcakes. For variety someone may bring fresh figs in the summer, venison sausage balls in the winter or king cakes (colorful New Orleans ring-shaped coffee cakes) during Mardi Gras season in February. There's a spontaneous flow of brotherly love. I can't imagine church without food and conversation afterward. If I had to do without it, I would feel deprived. The Bible describes such fellowship as part of the worship experience. "They devoted themselves to the apostles' teaching and to the fellowship, to the breaking of bread and to prayer," says Acts 2:42 of the early Christians.

In the South, rural areas like the one where I live tend to be loaded with churches. Unfortunately, they're also loaded with people who don't attend. My little church has done me as much good spiritually as regular exercise and a low-fat diet (church dinners excepted) do physically. It's unfortunate that more people don't partake. I can see why, though, when I think of all the negative stereotypes about churches: full of stick-in-the-mud, hypocritical, self-righteous members who look down their noses on others; preachers who either bore you to death or make you feel like a criminal bound for hell. But then I think of the positive traits I actually find: warm, supporting members who exhibit a spirit of selfless love; preachers who encourage my spirit to grow toward God. Churches like this can put our problems in perspective and remind us that there is more to life than we think, especially when we get bogged down in the daily grind.

Of course, churches aren't always places of peace. Sometimes factions develop, frequently over the smallest things. That Christians fail to honor Jesus' wish that we be as one reflects the negative side of human nature. But as I finished painting and went into the empty sanctuary, it occurred to me how fleeting such disputes are. They come and go, but the church still stands, quietly inviting, a place to worship God and fellowship with each other.

It's a place even an owl can go to find wisdom.

9

HOLY LAND,
SOUTHERN STYLE

The idea came to me in a burst of inspiration: canoe the Jordan River! What could be more natural for a guy whose job titles include religion editor and outdoors editor? for someone who loves to take long camping trips and is interested in all things biblical? Since canoeing is my preferred mode of transportation, paddling the Jordan, which runs through the very heart of the Holy Land, seemed like an ideal way to travel.

The standard tourist view of the Holy Land—or anywhere else, for that matter—doesn't grab me, you understand. When I go adventuring, I want to see backcountry. I feel like I don't know a place until I build a campfire, pitch a tent and gaze at the stars.

I started perusing maps and guidebooks. I learned that the Jordan has two sections, one stretching from the mountainous headwaters to the Sea of Galilee, the other going from the Sea of Galilee to the Dead Sea where the river ends. Much of the upper stretch is whitewater, more suited for rafts and kayaks than long-distance canoe touring. The slower parts are heavily used by tubers and canoe renters. The clear choice for me was the lower stretch, which passes the site of Jesus' baptism. That section is sixty-five miles as the crow flies and well over a hundred as the fish swims.

There were obvious problems, however. The river runs along the border between the nation of Jordan and land occupied by Israel. Jordan lies to the east while Israel holds the disputed West Bank. The region is full of soldiers and suicide bombers—hardly a typical canoeing destination. I called a local minister who has led numerous tours of the Holy Land. He referred me to an Israeli adventure outfitter in Florida, who in turn referred me to the Israel Department of Tourism, which has an office in Dallas. The folks there were enthusiastic about the concept—adventure travel with a religious angle! A new way to promote tourism! But they became dubious when I asked about logistics. After checking into it for me, a department spokesman said most of the river is too shallow to canoe. Besides, it turned out much of the lower Jordan was off-limits to the public for security reasons. Hmm. Uncanoeable and illegal.

Not one to take a government spokesman at face value, however, I consulted people who have lived and traveled in Israel. They concurred that the lower Jordan is inadequate for a canoe. Still not satisfied—since few people realize what a canoe can do—I read about some nineteenth-century journeys on the river. Two groups of explorers tried to float that segment and wound up dragging their boats and fighting rapids, which government officials say no longer even exist since the water flow is now controlled and used heavily for irrigation.

I briefly considered alternatives. The Tigris or Euphrates maybe? They're in Iraq—enough said. The Nile? Too big, and not really in the Holy Land. So my inspiration ran aground, for the time being anyway. But the experience turned my mind to my own region, in particular its similarities to the Holy Land. What I found surprised me.

There are huge differences, of course. The Middle East is mountains and desert, while the Deep South is lowlands and forest. But beyond those obvious contrasts lie some subtle likenesses. For instance:

- The Sea of Galilee, also known as the Sea of Tiberias, is the size of Louisiana's Lake Maurepas, while the Dead Sea is comparable to Lake Pontchartrain. There's even a Jordan River (sometimes spelled Jourdan) in south Mississippi. And the Gulf of Mexico compares to the Mediterranean Sea.

- The Holy Land has a strong rural tradition of fishing, herding and farming, much like the South.

- The centers of power, like Rome, Egypt and Jerusalem, lay far from Jesus' stomping grounds in Galilee. The rural Deep South is likewise a good piece from New York, Washington, even New Orleans.

- Jesus' hometown had a low reputation. "Nazareth! Can anything good come from there?" snorted a man named Nathanael in John 1:46. I hear the same attitude about Mississippi—ignorant, rural, racist rednecks.

- The South has had its share of civil strife—certainly not as bad as the thousands of years of factionalism in the Middle East, but pretty rough anyway.

When people want to become famous, they typically light out for destinations like New York or Hollywood. Most of Jesus' ministry, however, took place in small towns and rural areas. He never set foot in Rome, and he didn't go to Jerusalem until the end of his ministry. He was able to change the world from one of its remotest corners.

Christians often hunger to see the Holy Land in order to imagine what life in Jesus' time was like; I know I do. But we can do that right here. Picture him at a small-town church, at a state-park chapel, by the waterside at a popular fishing hole. Jesus recruited his disciples from among fishermen. In my local culture, I picture Jesus—in jeans, not a robe—at a lake in south Mississippi where some guys are fussing with lines in a flatbottom boat.

"Any luck?" he asks.

"Nope," allows one guy, spitting a stream of tobacco juice.

Jesus nods at a line of cypress trees. "Chunk a line out by that stump."

The guys stare at him, wondering whether to laugh. Then one of them shrugs, picks up a spinning rod and makes a long cast. Fish on! His buddies lunge for their rods, and in minutes the ice chests are full. They look over at Jesus and start to get an eerie feeling. This is no wandering bass pro. Unexpectedly, one of the men breaks into tears. And Jesus has his first disciples, just like in Luke 5:1-11.

I find something immensely comforting in all this. If rural areas like the Deep South ever seem to be benighted backwaters, as the world's opinion might suggest, well, so was Galilee. And if such a place was good enough for Jesus, it's more than good enough for me.

10

AMONG THE
MISKITO INDIANS

When Scott and I went to Honduras on a church mission trip in 1991, we were also scouting for future adventures in wild places. We soon learned about a region called La Mosquitia, a tropical wilderness spanning the eastern portions of Honduras and Nicaragua, a land of jungle, mountains, swamps, savannah and pine forests inhabited by Miskito Indians, along with jaguars, tapirs, monkeys and snakes. Later that year we made an exploratory trip there— enough to whet our appetite. What we really wanted to do was take a canoe all the way through Mosquitia, perhaps down the Patuca River, which slices it diagonally. But we saw no affordable way either to take a boat with us or to get hold of one there.

One winter day a few years later we were paddling Mississippi's Strong River, talking about Mosquitia, and I told Scott that if we could just find a portable vessel at an affordable price I'd be willing to go. A week later at the newspaper I got a letter from Scan-Sport Canoe Company offering to let me, as outdoors editor, test-paddle its sixteen-and-a-half-foot collapsible "pak-canoe." I called the owner, who was willing to let us take it down the Patuca.

Scott and I made plans in earnest. We would fly to La Ceiba, Honduras, travel via bush plane and truck to the village of Auasbila on the Coco River, then hire carriers and hike two days north through the rain forest to the Patuca. We would assemble the pak-canoe and paddle 120 miles northeast to the village of Brus Laguna near the coast, where there is a small airstrip.

When we got to Auasbila, Scott and I, who speak rudimentary Spanish, hired five Miskito carriers and a motorized dugout, then headed up the Coco. We reached the trail, loaded up and set off into the forest.

The banana jungle along the river soon gave way to virgin rain forest. Amazingly, the pass through the rugged Colon

Mountains was almost perfectly flat. But the sixteen-mile trail was far from easy. It was muddy despite the dry season, narrow and endlessly tricky with roots, vines and creeks. We camped at a stream halfway.

The next day the forest grew even wilder, with abundant jaguar and ocelot tracks and the plate-sized footprints of tapir. At times we glimpsed towering cliffs through the foliage. We reached the Patuca at mid-afternoon and assembled our red pak-canoe in thirty minutes. The men were impressed. One even took measurements with a stick so he could carve his own out of a log when he got back home.

Even so, they thought Scott and I were crazy to undertake the journey downriver. They told us we would face robbers, fierce headwinds, boat-swamping waves, rapids, crocodiles, deadly snakes and the possibility of sharks in the river. Soon our heads were swimming with worry.

"Dario," I said to the leader, who had remained quiet through the discussion, "your friends think this trip is very dangerous. What about you?"

"No," he said emphatically.

"Why not?"

"Because you believe in God." Then he turned the tables.

"What about you? What do you think?"

I was forced to choose between fear and faith on the spot. "I think God will protect us," I said—and ordered myself to believe it.

The next morning Scott and I said farewell to our guides, loaded our boat and set off down the wide, swift, muddy Patuca. Our plan was to follow the Patuca until it split near the coast. Then we would take the smaller Rio Amatingni through the marshes to the town of Brus Laguna.

We paddled in the shadow of misty, jungle-covered mountains, the air vibrant with exotic birdcalls. At the first village we stopped to buy coconuts, bows and arrows, and artwork made from tree bark. The inhabitants seemed friendly but reserved. They were hospitable, but in a lawless region like this, they were naturally wary of strangers.

We soon encountered the fierce headwinds our guides had spoken of. They arrived around three p.m.—as they would every day of our float—as if someone had switched on a giant fan. As we paddled we saw whitecaps appear up ahead; minutes later the blast struck us head-on. We immediately looked for a place to camp but had to struggle for quite a while before a suitable site appeared.

The next day the mountains gave way to jungle-covered

lowlands. We camped in the jungle and on sandbars, stopping at villages occasionally, chatting with Indians along the way. Mosquitia, though tropical, is geographically similar to much of the Deep South. Dense jungle lines muddy brown rivers, with pine savannah farther inland. Native American tribes once lived along rivers in the South much as the Miskitos and Sumos do along the Patuca, hunting, fishing and gardening, traveling by foot and canoe.

Of course, the Patuca is not untouched by progress. Many people have guns, either .22-caliber rifles or AK-47s left over from the Nicaraguan revolution. There are a few outboard motors on the rivers as well, and two or three villages have bush airstrips where small planes can land. But otherwise it's just woods and river.

On our last evening before turning onto Rio Amatingni, we made camp on a muddy sandbar. After supper we sat outside the tent and laughed about all the dangers that had not come to pass. Then two men in a dugout landed. One of them, dressed in rags and carrying an AK-47, gave our gear a close look. "You have a lot of equipment," he said.

"Not so much," I hastened to say.

Then Scott said, "Would you like a cigar?"

The expression on the man's face brightened. *"Si!"* He lit

the cigar, whistled to his hunting dogs and went on up the sandbar to hunt for turtle eggs.

Shortly afterward a ferocious swarm of mosquitoes arrived. In our mad dash to get into the tent we broke the zipper and had to cram clothes against the opening. Countless mosquitoes got inside in the meantime. Despite the unbelievable horde outside, we saw the two visitors paddle away, unprotected, in the gloom.

The next day we turned left onto the Rio Amatingni, albeit with some misgivings. While most people had told us the route would be clear all the way to Brus Laguna, one man warned us that finding our way would be nearly impossible without a guide. What we didn't expect was for the Rio Amatingni to dry up—yet that's exactly what happened.

A muddy riverbed gridlocked with logs stretched as far as we could see. We knew it was the dry season, but we had no idea its effects could be so drastic. Portaging was out of the question. Yet behind us lay the prospect of days of paddling back upstream against the current.

We found an Indian man burning off some ground for crops on the riverbank and asked his advice. He said there was a back way to Brus Laguna and drew us a crude map showing a narrow channel stitching several lakes together. I didn't see how we could find our way through such a maze in a swamp larger than the Everglades, but we had little choice. I said a silent prayer as Scott and I turned off on the designated route, a ditch little wider than our canoe.

A cool Caribbean breeze blew across a gorgeous expanse of marsh reaching to the horizon, dotted with abundant bird life, from pink flamingoes to giant storks. This was desolate, magical country. The channel emptied into a small lake, and we paddled across and found another channel, just as the man had told us. I stood up in the stern and saw a low range of blue mountains probably fifty miles to the north. My fears gave way to a rare sense of freedom. I felt like I was flying.

On the second lake we met a dugout and got more directions. The third lake, nearly a mile across, was more problematic as we battled wind, waves and mud flats. I could smell the sea in the wind that gusted across the grass. We took a wrong turn into a dead-end cove before spotting a dugout emerging from the correct channel.

After hours of paddling we saw houses on stilts with rusty metal roofs: Brus Laguna. The little town, with no roads in or out, was hardly modern, but there was a generator, two or three trucks and a tiny airstrip. A local family, recommended by missionaries, provided us with food, lodging and help getting out.

Days later, flying home from Honduras, I reflected on the lesson of faith I learned from Dario, the beauty of nature, the generosity of strangers and, most of all, the guidance of God. For more than a week after I got home, I dreamed nightly that I was still gliding through the marshes and lagoons of La Mosquitia.

II

—

RIVERBANK WORSHIP

I used to consider weekend camping trips and Sunday morning worship mutually exclusive. I either did one or the other. And since I'm an avid outdoorsman, that meant spending many Sundays without worship (though, admittedly, being outdoors can be a religious experience). That changed in Oregon, and not through my own initiative.

I was camping with five other guys, not all of them Christians, when on Sunday morning my brother Robert said to me, "How about giving us a sermon?" I was taken aback. I mustered a few sentences about how grateful we should be to the Creator for the wonderful nature all around. My expectant audience looked disappointed. "That's all?" Robert said in the blunt manner to which big brothers are prone.

Next time around I was prepared. It was a spring canoe trip on Mississippi's Yazoo River. I was with three other guys, two of whose religious beliefs I knew nothing about. Sunday morning by the campfire I pulled out the little New Testament with Psalms and Proverbs that I carry on trips. "It's Sunday morning," I declared. "How about I read some Scripture?"

They were agreeable. I opened to Psalm 104, one of my favorites of the many passages in the Bible that extol the wonders of God's creation. As I read "He stretches out his heavens like a tent," I became aware of the blue, cloud-dappled sky.

The birds of the air nest by the waters;
    they sing among the branches.

Birds twittered all around us in the woods as if to demonstrate.

The trees of the Lord are well watered.

Indeed they were, in this case by the nearby Yazoo.

You bring darkness, it becomes night,
    and all the beasts of the forest prowl.

I thought of the coyotes I'd heard the night before, not far from camp.

The sun rises, and they steal away.

Bars of sunlight sloped into the misty woods.

How many are your works, O LORD!

Amen and amen. When I finished reading the chapter, I felt uplifted and inspired. My audience seemed to appreciate it as much as I did. Sunday morning campfire Bible reading was okay, I decided.

On an autumn trip down Louisiana's Atchafalaya River, I extended the idea even further. I suggested to my companion Steve Cox, a fellow Christian, that we each pick out a favorite Scripture passage and read it aloud. I chose Psalm 91 ("If you make the Most High your dwelling . . . / no disaster will come near your tent"). Steve responded with the Twenty-Third Psalm ("He leads me beside quiet waters, / he restores my soul"). Then Steve suggested we each pick a passage from the New Testament. He kicked off with I Corinthians 13 ("Love is patient, love is kind"). I countered with Luke 5:1-11 ("Then he sat down and taught the people from the boat"). And we were ready to start the day.

When Steve and I floated Mississippi's Chunky River, we again selected passages of Scripture to read on Sunday morning. He chose Ephesians 3: "Although I am less than the least of all God's people, this grace was given me: to preach to the Gentiles the unsearchable riches of Christ, and to make plain to everyone the administration of this mystery, which for ages past was kept hidden in God, who created all things." That's food for thought when you're sitting on a sandbar with the rising sun behind you and a grove of young fall-tinged birches glimmering across a chuckling river. "The unsearchable riches of Christ . . ."

For my turn, I chose Psalm 1:

Blessed is the man
    who does not walk in the counsel of the wicked
or stand in the way of sinners
    or sit in the seat of mockers.
But his delight is in the law of the LORD,
    and on his law he meditates day and night.
He is like a tree planted by streams of water,
    which yields its fruit in season
and whose leaf does not wither.

I looked down the sandbar to a persimmon thicket where

the small orange fruit dangled, not quite in season yet. Beyond them the river glistened in brisk sunlight. Now that's a good way to observe a Sunday morning outdoors.

I feel compelled to point out that the outdoors can't take the place of church—though it took me a while to arrive at that conclusion. When editor Charles Dunagin interviewed me for a newspaper reporting job in 1979, he asked me what, if any, church I attended. "The church of the woods," I retorted. Dunagin was unimpressed. What I didn't know at the time was that he was not only a devout churchgoer but a passionate quail hunter, well acquainted with the glories of nature. And he knew that the outdoors is no substitute for church. Since then I too have become a churchgoer (ironically, at a church named Woodland). And while I continue to experience God outdoors, I've come to agree with Dunagin.

Folks who claim the outdoors can take the place of church may not actually spend their outdoor time in worship. They're probably busy hunting, fishing, canoeing. I know that's how it was for me during the years when I regularly missed church during deer season. On Sunday morning I was watching for antlers, not pondering ways to serve God and fellow humans, lifting my voice in praise, or seeking spiritual instruction. The Bible is full of praise for the wonders of nature, and characters from Moses to Elijah to Jesus routinely went off into the wilderness to commune with God—but not to the exclusion of temple or church.

Church offers some things the woods can't deliver. We gather with fellow believers or seekers, hopefully experiencing a sense of love and communion we can't get anywhere else. We praise God by singing, communicate with him by praying. We listen to a sermon, read the Bible and discuss a lesson in Sunday school, all of which is meant to broaden our understanding of God and his world. We partake of holy Communion, symbolizing an unfathomable sacrifice.

But this doesn't mean you won't find me camping out on several weekends throughout the year. A working man sometimes has to take his outings on weekends, and I don't think God will fault me for retreating to the wilderness now and then.

12

MOUNTAIN MEN

I'm not the only person who thinks religion and the outdoors mix easily. Roger and Grant Lewis, two grizzled brothers from Lincoln County, Mississippi, are as comfortable talking about prayer and angels as they are discussing catfish and deer. When they're holed up in their camp, their stories conjure up mysteries as deep as the woods around them.

"Ever feel like you were born out of time?" Grant mused when I visited them at their hunting club one dark, cold, rainy spring day. The camp consisted of a couple of small trailers and a shed with a tin roof, black plastic on two sides and an iron barrel woodheater in the center. On this dreary day the fire in the heater felt just right.

The Lewis brothers would have fit right in around, say, 1840, somewhere west of the Missouri Breaks. Both sport burly beards. Roger's is white, and the kids at Mount Gilead Primitive Baptist Church think he's Santa Claus incarnate. Grant's black beard and intense, dark eyes make him look like he just rode down from the high sierra for a rendezvous. These are Mississippi-style mountain men, top-notch woodsmen who have dropped many a buck with arrows and grabbed catfish writhing from deep holes. And they don't drink, smoke or cuss. But it wasn't always that way.

Roger was sitting in a bar several years ago "waiting for the party to happen" when an unexpected wave of disgust swept over him. Until then, he says, he could down a fifth of whisky in a twinkling and you'd never know it. On this particular evening the liquor didn't taste right.

The party started, but Roger left. Shortly thereafter he went to church and heard the story of the prodigal son. He knew then that he had come home. "A beer or a highball won't send you to hell, but it can make your life hell," Roger said.

Grant's conversion came later. "I spent forty years wandering in the wilderness," he says, referring to weekends lost in an alcoholic fog. One Sunday he lay morosely on the couch watching a Billy Graham special. As he watched the crowds pour forth to be saved, his own emotions stirred. Later, at Praise Cathedral Church of God, he was smitten by the Spirit.

"I got dizzy and my knees got weak," Grant recalled.

He quit drinking immediately. Smoking took a bit longer to put down. For a three-pack-a-day man, it took some hard praying.

Now at their hunting club the strongest drink served is black coffee. During my visit, Grant kept the fire stoked while Roger brewed coffee in his treasured, well-seasoned pot. "It'll put hair on your chest," he said. The brew was strong, black and good, its smell mixed with that of wood smoke and wet dog. Poncho, Roger's big black mix of rottweiler, Doberman and German shepherd, dozed under a table.

Grant recalled a fishing trip on Bayou Pierre when he brought small mudcats (bullhead catfish) for bait while Roger brought shiners (minnows) in a plastic bag. Roger sneered at Grant's choice of mudcats—until he released his shiners into a mesh container and they escaped through the gaps. That left the brothers with half a dozen mudcat and tiny No. 2 hooks.

They baited the trotline and were camped on a sandbar near it when *galoosh!*—something big hit. Grant pulled up a straightened hook. The action had begun. "I was wishing for more mudcat then," Roger said with a laugh. They landed some big fish that night.

Talk of fish and game gave way to stories of prayer, angels, visions and miracles. These men's minds turn to God just as truly as Roger's arrows have downed one hundred or so deer.

Their hunting club land winds along the south bank of the Homochitto River, and when the rain let up, Roger gave me a tour. The Lewises had their camp right on the river till high water flooded it and claimed Grant's canoe. They still walk to the spot to fish in a hole equally popular with cottonmouth snakes. Back off the river, we walked a lane beneath giant overcup oaks, gnarly cypress, eager young poplars and fragrant sassafras. A gray-dark deer slipped across the road, and Poncho tore out in a frenzy but soon returned, not enough hound blood in him to sustain a chase. The trail circled back toward camp, passing an artesian well where water shot out of a white plastic pipe, cool and woods-sweet.

In their conversion from rough-living backwoodsmen to passionate Christians, Roger and Grant carried on a tradition with roots in the American frontier. Religious revivals swept the frontier in the late 1700s and early 1800s. One missionary active then was William Winans, Methodist circuit rider in southwest Mississippi. In fact, Winans trod the same paths the Lewises do today. "Extensive rivers, creeks, swamps, and canebrakes made travel on Claiborne (circuit) difficult and sometimes dangerous," writes Ray Holder in *William Winans: Methodist Leader in Antebellum Mississippi* (University Press of Mississippi, 1977). "Ferries operated on Big and Little Bayou Pierre and Big Black, but not on their tributaries."

Winans and his fellow preachers encountered plenty of hard-drinking backwoodsmen. "The 'greatest rudeness' which Winans and Paine encountered along 'The Devil's Backbone' was from white men at taverns," Holder writes.

Thanks largely to efforts of Winans and others like him, the rural South is now liberally sprinkled with churches. But "you can go to church all your life and not be saved," Grant said. He admitted he doesn't like to preach too much, though. In that respect, he said, religion is like fishing: "How many fish have you ever scared into a boat?"

13

GOD SPEAKS

I was standing on the bank of Mississippi's Little Sunflower River when I heard God speak. It was a drizzly September morning, and I was waiting for a ride after a camping trip. I stood in wet grass staring idly at the big woods, my thoughts rambling in a holy direction since it was a Sunday. Then a gust of wind stirred the treetops, and my ears came alive.

I suddenly became aware of the sounds: raindrops pattering on the river and hissing in the grass; runoff water gurgling into the whispering river; crows and other birds vocalizing despite the weather; and of course the wind whooshing through the treetops. All these sounds that we take for granted—where do they come from? The wind stirred again and an answer formed in my mind: God.

The prevailing wisdom is that God is silent, that he spoke to the Old Testament prophets but doesn't speak anymore. But maybe, as a contemporary Christian song declares, "He is not silent; we are not listening." Who says God must speak in English? Why should he confine the infinite range of his voice to puny words? The sounds of Little Sunflower River were more than voices. They were a grand symphony whose fluid combinations made Mozart seem absurdly primitive.

For that matter, it seems silly to compare them to Mozart at all. We humans instinctively imagine we're the be-all and end-all of creation, the standard by which all else is measured. If that's so, why did God create so many wonders we'll never witness? We'll never see all the stellar wonders millions of light years away. We'll never examine each intricate pebble on the bed of a nearby creek. So why did God bother to invent them?

Maybe he delights in his handiwork in the same way we enjoy our gardens and flower beds. That particularly struck me one summer day flying home from Michigan. Right at sunset the plane began to descend toward the cloud banks.

Those ruffled, furrowed cloud tops ranged from deep blue in the shadows to silver and gold and a brilliance of color that has no name unless it be pure light. Like day lilies, those clouds were in constant flux, here today, gone tomorrow. Perhaps God was bending over that field of cloud blossoms like my wife bends over the mass of white clematis blooming on our deck. Angelyn likes visitors to appreciate the flowers, but she doesn't rely on them for her own enjoyment. God wants us to recognize the glory of his creation, but it's presumptuous to suppose our appreciation is the only reason for the creation.

We are coarse, dull, brutish creatures. While we occasionally pause to sniff the flowers, we are much more practiced in concentrating on our petty problems and plans. Meanwhile a divine symphony is in full concert all around us. And it doesn't always take place in exotic or wilderness settings: the prettiest sunset I ever saw was from the parking lot of a local shopping center.

Angelyn and our son Andy were in a store while I, who hate shopping, stayed outside in the pickup truck. Sitting bored in the driver's seat, I watched in growing amazement as the humdrum parking-lot sky turned into an explosion of reds, blues and everything in between. It was absolutely astonishing, and it shattered my notion that the best sunsets take place in romantic environments like beaches or mountains.

Beaches and mountains are mere backdrops when it comes to sunsets. A sunset is not tethered to geography— nor are the wonders of creation. God is nondiscriminatory when it comes to displaying his works. Every facet of nature is his. Tundra, mountains, rocky sea coasts, rolling prairies, level plains, desert, hills, woods, swamp, marsh, rivers, lakes, bayous, jungle, rain forest, savannah, glaciers. Hot weather, cold, cool, warm, rain, sleet, ice, snow, steam, fog, sunshine and cloud. The best season is any season, the finest weather any weather. You don't have to go to Hawaii, Alaska or the Amazon to find the marvels of nature. They're everywhere we look, if we have the eyes to see.

Even in cities—where human invention has crowded out God's creation, or tried to anyway—nature elbows its way in: wildflowers in concrete, hawks on skyscrapers, birdsong above traffic noise. When a friend took me to an overlook at Fort Worth, Texas, one night, the lights of the city spread below us like a galaxy. Lovelier still is a balanced blend of human and divine handiwork: pastures, farms, orchards, yards and towns that leave room for woods and wildlife.

In wildlife, too, God shows no favoritism. An article

about an educational television special on chickens contends they are as majestic as any other creature. A possum is as marvelous as a rhinoceros if we have an eye for detail, a minnow as stunning as a whale. A pink-topped mushroom that grows overnight and lasts a week is as intricate as a two-thousand-year-old redwood.

A county park near my home in Mississippi is as awesome as the Rocky Mountains. It lacks snow-capped peaks but contains trees so tall you may wrench your neck staring, sloughs as dark as mirrors in an old house, a river that pipes like an orchestra of bamboo flutes, husky-throated owls, white-tailed-flashing deer, industrious squirrels, stately egrets.

Several passages in the Bible indicate the universal glory of creation. Psalm 148 urges everything and everyone to praise the Lord: "lightning and hail, snow and clouds, stormy winds that do his bidding, you mountains and all hills, fruit trees and all cedars, wild animals and all cattle, small creatures and flying birds, kings of the earth and all nations." But like Adam and Eve, we continually fail to get it. They had to try the one apple that was prohibited, not satisfied with all the other fruit. Solomon "denied myself nothing my eyes desired" only to find "everything was meaningless, a chasing after the wind" (Ecclesiastes 2:10, 11).

He had failed to see what was right in front of him. When he finally learned his lesson, he offered this advice: "Remember your Creator." If we do that, we'll be more likely to appreciate his handiwork all around, right before our eyes. We may even hear him speak.